For Felix Hilton
N.B.

· — · —

For Vickie
P.M.

First published 1987 by
Walker Books Ltd
87 Vauxhall Walk
London SE11 5HJ

Text © 1987 Paul Manning
Illustrations © 1987 Nicola Bayley

First printed 1987   Reprinted 1988
Printed and bound in Italy by L.E.G.O., Vicenza

British Library Cataloguing in Publication Data
Manning, Paul
Boy. – (Merry-go-rhymes)
I. Title   II. Bayley, Nicola   III. Series
821'.914   PZ8.3
ISBN 0-7445-0745-6

·BOY·

Written by
PAUL MANNING

Illustrated by
NICOLA BAYLEY

WALKER BOOKS
LONDON

Early
morning,
boy
yawning.

Bad luck,
head stuck.

Boy
slopping,
cup
dropping.

Clothes
drying,
boy
crying.

Sister
pushing,
boy
whooshing.

On the rug,
nice and
snug.

Father
washing,
boy
sploshing.

Sleepyhead,
time
for bed.